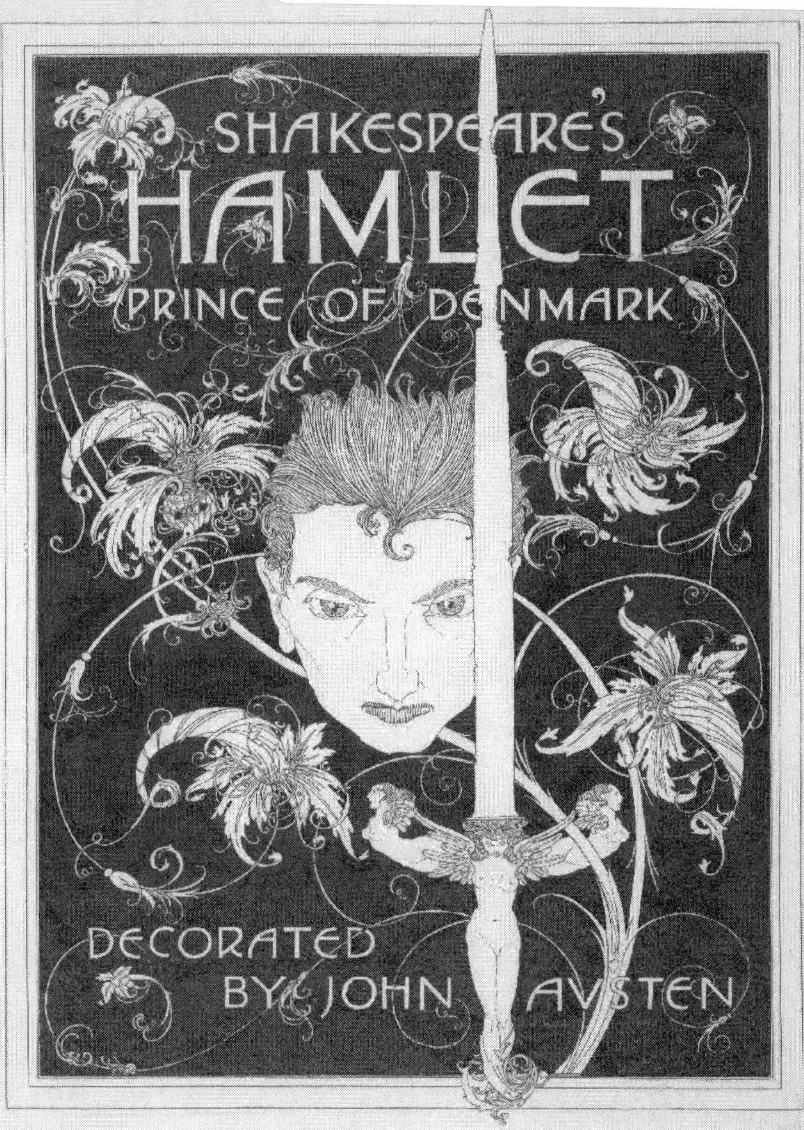
SHAKESPEARE'S
HAMLET
PRINCE OF DENMARK
DECORATED
BY JOHN AUSTEN

Get exclusive Millennial Shakespeare content

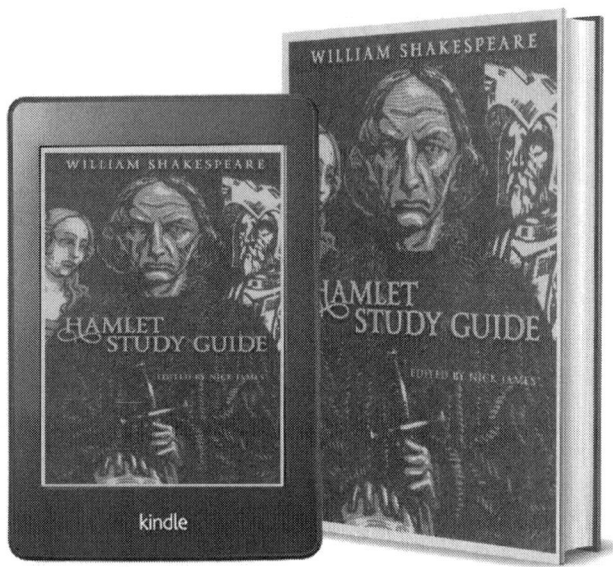

Building relationships with our readers is the very best thing about writing, according to the Millennial Shakespeare crew. That's why we occasionally like to send out newsletters with details on new releases, special offers, contests, and other information relating to the Millennial Shakespeare series. We don't want you to miss out on anything!

If you sign up to the mailing list today, you'll receive a few things we think you'll like:

- The Hamlet Study Guide, which includes a scene by scene breakdown of what happened in Hamlet
- A desktop background from John Austen, the premier illustrator of Shakespeare's plays
- Updates when a new Millennial Translation will be released AND a free Study Guide to accompany the release

You can get all this by signing up for our email list at www.millennialshakespeare.com. Hurry so you don't miss out!

Hamlet
By William Shakespeare
Characters in the Play

GHOST KING, Hamlet's dad and generally spooky dude
HAMLET, the straight up hero of the play, son of the late King Hamlet and Queen Gertrude
QUEEN, widow of King Hamlet, now married to a thot
THOT KING, basically a representation of the worst person you have ever met.

OPHELIA, Hamlet's wannabe side piece
LAERTES, her brother and general bad ass
POLONIUS, a weasel and father to Ophelia and Laertes
REYNALDO, much less important than his placement would suggest

HORATIO, Hamlet's bae and cool dude

Randos at the Danish court:
- **VOLTEMAND**
- **CORNELIUS**
- **ROSENCRANTZ**
- **GUILDENSTERN**
- **OSRIC**
- **Gentlemen**
- **A Lord**

Danish soldiers:
- **FRANCISCO**
- **BARDNARDO**
- **MARCELLUS**

FORINTBRAS, Prince of Norway
A Captain in Fortinbras's army

Ambassadors to Denmark from England

Players who take roles of **Prologue, Player King, Player Queen, and Lucianus** in *The Murder of Gonzago*

Two Messengers
Sailors
Gravedigger
Gravedigger's companion
Doctor of Divinity
Attendants, Lords, Guards, Musicians, Laertes's Followers, Soldiers, Officers.

ACT 1
Scene 1 Recap

A guard, Bernardo, relives another guard, Francisco, of his shift and invites two people, Marcellus and Horatio, to hang out with him during his shift. Marcellus is a guard and Horatio is a nobleman.

The two guards, Bernardo and Marcellus, have seen a ghost and then told Horatio about it. Horatio, the nobleman, doesn't believe it, at all, and kinda mocks them for believing in ghost. The two guards tell Horatio that is it real and he is going to be scared when he sees it. He is all "yeah okay" in his most sarcastic tone, but when a ghost DOES show up and Horatio almost goes all brown pants. Marcellus teases Horatio and convinces him into speaking with the ghost which he does, but the ghost doesn't speak back, probably because it's a ghost and they don't speak unless you have a recorder and get an EVP or something like that.

The two guards continue to mock Horatio for being scared and then get serious asking him if he thought it looked like the king that died before the play began. Horatio is all, yeah it totally does. Marcellus then ask Horatio to start a flashback so he and I suppose us, can understand the backstory of the play so we can find the story more intriguing.

Horatio tells him that Denmark was at war with Norway. Why Marcellus, a guard of Denmark doesn't know this idk. Anyway, Norway was the one who attacked first and Denmark was just defending themselves. During the war, the King of Norway signed to a contract saying that if he was defeated then all of Norway would then be owned by Denmark.

It wasn't a good plan, and sure enough Hamlet kills the king of Norway, earning all of Norway for Denmark. Well the king's son, I assumed named Joffrey, rejects the contract and forms a gang of hooligans to attack Denmark to reclaim Norway. This is why we have the guards in the beginning of the play watching over everything. It also is a way to introduce Hamlet and show that he is a bad ass.

Anyway, the ghost returns and Horatio being brave tries to talk to the ghost again. Marcellus tries to sneak up on the ghost...and stab it, but can't, probably because it's a ghost. These guys don't know jack about ghost. To be fair this is set between 1300-1500 AD, and Ghost Hunters would not be on tv for another 5 to 7 hundred years. Anyway, the ghost leaves after they try killing it, which is hysterical. They all regroup and decide to go tell Hamlet. Then the scene ends.

Scene 2 Recap

We start the scene with many important characters hanging out. Keep your eye on the THOT King, the Queen, Polonius, and Ophelia, they are all main characters. Shakespeare tends to introduce characters that don't actually mean anything, but they seem important at first. I think the role was written for someone important or who help fund the play, but that is just speculation on my part.

Ophelia isn't listed as a character in the scene or has any lines, but most adaptions place her in the scene. The THOT King's real name is Claudius. Some versions just call him by his name, but Shakespeare calls him as King, so we will do the same.

Anyway, he is giving a speech in the beginning of the scene. It starts off saying how sad it is they have lost their previous king, his brother, and he understands how everyone is in morning, but through that mourning they should rejoice for he married the Queen and is now King himself. He then recaps what we learned in the previous scene in new detail. We relearn that the young Fortinbras wants the lands his father lost in war returned to Norway. THOT King doesn't want to give them back and is writing to his Fortinbras' uncle telling him so. He then sends two people to deliver the news to the uncle.

THOT King turns his attention then to Laertes and ask what he wanted before the scene began. Laertes says he was only in Denmark to see a thot crowned king and now that's over he wants to go back to France. Ou la la. The King ask if Laertes has asked his dad's permission, because that's a thing a 20 something in 13th century Denmark did. Polonius, Laertes' father, makes a dad joke about how his son wore him down to a yes. The King then grants Laertes permission to leave and turns his attention to Hamlet. I am not going to retell the joke here because it is not funny, but clearly Polonius thinks it is.

Hamlet is moody, and it is so obvi to everyone. The Queen, Hamlet's mother, ask him to cheer up and reminds him that all fathers die like that is supposed to make him feel better. For whatever reason, Hamlet agrees with her. Then Queen presses why he is upset because she just rationalized his emotion away and expects him to immediately be happy.

Hamlet goes on this emo rant about why it doesn't SEEM he is upset mother; he is upset mother. The THOT King steeps in and basically tells Hamlet to get over it and he is being a wuss. The THOT King is dick. THOT King goes off on why Hamlet needs to man up, then tells Hamlet he doesn't want him to go to school in Wittenberg, Germany and that he is his daddy now. The Queen also pleads with Hamlet not to leave Elsinore Denmark. Hamlet agrees to stay. This makes the THOT King happy with Hamlet's response and commands everyone to leave for reasons.

Hamlet pulls out his diary, I assume, and starts writing an emo poem. He wants his flesh to melt off and turn into a dew or puddle and wonders why God doesn't like suicide. Then he doesn't see any joy in the world and how it is all just a garden filled with weeds. He turns to thoughts on his father and how he died two months ago. His mother then remarried shortly afterwards which confuses Hamlet because he thought his mom was obsessed with his father. He doesn't understand why she would fall for his uncle. Hamlet has this image of his dad as being this great man, and his uncle is a shady snake.

Horatio, Marcellus, and Bernardo enter and after some greeting, they tell Hamlet about seeing his dad's ghost. Hamlet questions them about it and finds out that it has appeared three times in a row. He asks if they will be on guard tonight and they say they will be. Hamlet then says he will hang out with them to see if he can see the ghost. He kind of invites himself to go to their job, but none of them object. Hamlet ends the scene thinking something bad must of happened to his dad.

Scene 3 Recap

Laertes is with Ophelia right before he is about to depart for France. He first asks his sister to write him letters while he is away, and she says of course she will. Laertes then changes the subject to Hamlet. He is concerned that his sister will fall for Hamlet and it will only end in heartbreak for her. He reminds her that Hamlet as a Prince and can love who he wants, but when he becomes king, he may have to marry someone for the benefit of the crown, and she will be left in the cold. Ophelia tells her brother she understands but he can't be asking her to stick to the rivers and lakes she is used to when he is out chasing waterfalls himself. They laugh at her response as siblings do. Then their father enters.

Polonius is very nice to Laertes and gives him some fatherly advice. Pretty standard stuff. Don't be a fool or getting into trouble because you friends are being stupid. He does tell him to dress nice, he is going to France after all. Laertes thanks his father for the advice and tells Ophelia to remember what he told her. She delivers a great line "'Tis in my memory locked, and you yourself shall keep the key of it."

Polonius then turns his attention to Ophelia and her affections towards Hamlet. He does not approve. She tries to convince her father that Hamlet is bae, but he is being stubborn and thinks he knows what's best for her. He forbids Ophelia from seeing Hamlet again and the scene ends.

Scene 4 Recap

Hamlet, Horatio, and Marcellus arrive at the guard post. Hamlet realizes that it's really really cold up there and wonders what time it is. Marcellus says it's after midnight and Horatio says it's around the time the ghost usually shows up being all spooky. Horatio hears a band playing in the distance and asks Hamlet what it means.

Hamlet explains that it is the THOT King up partying late into the night. Hamlet explains this is a new tradition in Denmark; one he does not like. Other countries think Denmark is full of drunks now and it is taking away from their many military and social accomplishments. He also comments on how some people are born to be drunks and it's not their fault. However, he does see good men get drunk and do foolish things.

The ghost enters, and Hamlet tries talking to it. Does no one in Denmark know that ghost don't talk! He calls out to the ghost but there is no answer until the ghost motions for Hamlet to follow. His friends are all "hell nah" but Hamlet is all "yeah brah". There is a little bit of a fight between them and Hamlet eventually gets away and following the ghost. Marcellus says the famous line "Something is rotten in the state of Denmark." Remember it's Marcellus who says it as it could be on a test or trivia question one day.

Scene 5 Recap

This is a crazy scene fyi! Hamlet and the speaking ghost. I've heard of ghost giving EVPs but not soliloquies. Anyway, that's Shakespeare. He has some crazy stuff and I think it is only going to get crazier as we get further into this play.

Hamlet is following the ghost and then gives up and demands the ghost stop and speak. The ghost immediately speaks telling him that he doesn't have much time before he has to return to be tortured by...fire. Sounds like a good time, I don't know why he wouldn't want to get back to that ASAP.

The ghost warns Hamlet that if he tells him what he wants then Hamlet will want revenge. The ghost then goes on and tells him that he is his father's ghost or spirit. He is cursed to walk the night for a "certain term" and then in the day be consumed by fire until all of his sins are burned away. So basically, not yoga. He is also forbidden to tell Hamlet any of the details of what I assume is hell. He then goes on a super dark description of what will happen to Hamlet if the ghost tells him about hell and ends asking if Hamlet ever loved his dad. It is a weird transition.

Hamlet replies "Oh God" probably because his mind was just blown right then. The ghost tells Hamlet that he was murdered, and Hamlet immediately swears revenge. The ghost tells Hamlet that he was sleeping in his orchard when a serpent stung him, and that serpent was Hamlet's Uncle! Dun Dun Dun. I also think it's funny how he doesn't call out his brother by name, but basically calls him a snake. I guess if my brother killed me, I wouldn't use his name either. Hey bro, love ya, don't kill me okay?

Anyway, the ghost goes into a long monologue about how his brother is evil but knows how to seduce women, and how he seduced his wife, who he thought really loved him. It's sad. He loved her so much and thought she was going to Notebook him back, but instead she jumps in bed with an everyday thot, and the worse part of it is, his brother isn't half the man he was. He was Kobe beef and now she is settling for a thrown out hot dog. Despite that he asks Hamlet not to judge or seek revenge on his mom. She will pay for her sins when she dies. He then says goodbye 3 times and skedaddles. Hamlet is taken back by the experience, understandably so. He takes a moment and then starts to form a plan. He is going to forget everything else in life and only focus on this. He also can't believe his mother.

His buddies show up and wake him up out a daze. They ask him to tell them what happened, and he is being coy about it. Also, weren't they supposed to be following him and stay in the corner. What happened there? Did they lose him in the bushes or something? We don't get that answer. Hamlet admits there is a villain in Denmark and Horatio is like "we knew that, we didn't need a ghost to tell us." Then Hamlet says some crazy stuff and Horatio immediately calls him out on it. Hamlet apologizes for any offense and Horatio says there is none, but Hamlet counters saying there is Offense! He must be a difficult friend to have.

He wants them to swear to him that they won't say anything about what they saw during the night and they swear. He then doubles down and ask them to swear on his sword. They are confused as they just swore but Hamlet insist and then the ghost starts yelling at them to swear as well from underneath the stage. There is a back and forth, but they swear. Hamlet tells them that he is going to start acting crazy and they cannot tell anyone that this is all a trick. He isn't really mad; he is just acting mad. They agree, and the scene ends.

From this point on in the play you have to decide if Hamlet is really mad or if he is just acting crazy. There is no right or wrong. Many people debate his madness. Ghost don't usually talk to people and Hamlet could of imagined it all. Plus, his friends couldn't find him during the EVP session he had with his dead dad and when they did find him, he was acting all weird.

On the other hand, he did see his dead dad and his ghost daddy told him he was murdered by his Uncle and asked him to avenge his death. If that happened then Hamlet isn't mad, just acting loony. You will have to decide, but what is pretty clear is that Hamlet really is the First Avenger, not Captain America.

End of Act One

ACT 2
Scene 1 Recap

Polonius is with his servant Reynaldo in his office. He gives Reynaldo money and messages to give to his son Laertes in France. Then Polonius ask Reynaldo when he gets to Paris to find out if there are other Danish people there and to find out about them. Are they rich? Why are they in Paris? And if so, do they know his son? He asks Reynaldo to find out what his son has been up. For example, has he been out drinking and having sex with prostitutes? This is literally what Polonius ask Reynaldo to find out and to ask people this.

Reynaldo is surprised at this request and ask if this won't ruin his honor and respect in polite society. It's a fair point. Polonius clarifies that he only wants to ask that if it comes up in natural conversation. He goes on telling Reynaldo to lie about his son, Laertes, but only to gain the trust of the people he is speaking to, in hopes, that then they will be truthful about his son's actions. This goes back on forth a little bit until Reynaldo figures out his goal is to find out if Laertes is partying and being a general fool like a rich kid in Paris would probably do or is, he just studying music like he is supposed to do. No matter what he finds out from the rumor mill he is then supposed to confirm it with his own eyes. He leaves, and Ophelia enters.

Ophelia is a little bit freaked out over her last meeting with Hamlet. He showed up wrecked and completely disheveled. His jacket was unbuttoned, his socks were dirty, and he wasn't wearing a hat...he wasn't even wearing...a hat! Ophelia is having none of it and is outta there, leaving the hatless Hamlet.

Hamlet grabbed Ophelia's arm and stared at her face as if he was Jack wanting to draw Rose on the Titanic. Polonius thinks this story shows that Hamlet is madly in love with Ophelia, and by madly in love he means mad because he loves her. He is literally crazy because of his feelings for Ophelia. He concludes that they have to go to the thot King and tell him about how Hamlet has been acting. Ophelia agrees, and they go.

Was Hamlet acting crazy like he said he was going to do in the previous seen or he is actually crazy? I don't know. I suspect he is acting right now.

Also, is it just me or is Polonius a jerk? He tells his son to go and have fun, engage in youthful activities and then turns around and is super mean to his daughter for liking Hamlet, a handsome and rich battle proven Prince. Polonius goes so far as to forbidding her from seeing him.

In this very scene with Polonius pays a dude to go spy on his son and to tell lies about his son to gain the trust of his strangers...and Hamlet is the one to not be trusted. Also, with Ophelia he thinks that Hamlet is madly in love, by that I mean he is crazy, and runs off to go tell the King, not because he is endangering his daughter, but to win favor with the thot King. If this was Game of Thrones, then he would be Joffrey without the crown. He is just a jerk. F' him. I don't like him. Someone invite him to a Purple Wedding ASAP.

Scene 2 Recap

Okay this is a long one. 634 lines or 15% of the entire play. Reading line by line takes about 30 minutes and some of the film versions of this scene takes just as long if not longer. With all that being said, let's dive into the final scene of Act 2.

We start with the Thot King and Queen in their throne room welcoming Guildenstern and Rosencrantz, as a side note you have to go watch "Guildenstern and Rosencrantz Are Dead" it's hysterical and worth watching Tim Roth and Gary Oldman play these characters. Anyway, the thot King and Queen brought them to court to find out what is going on with Hamlet. Is he crazy? If so why? What is making him crazy? Guildenstern and Rosencrantz are two of Hamlet's closest and longest friends, being friends since childhood. They figure if anyone can find out the truth then they can. It's a fair assumption. Guildenstern and Rosencrantz agree and leave.

Polonius, the jerk face, enters with news that the messenger they sent to Norway has return. He also says he thinks he knows why Hamlet is President of the Looney bin but wants to tell the thot King and Queen after the Norway messenger delivers his news first. Polonius leaves to go get the messenger.

There are technically 2 messengers but only one of them speaks. I don't know why Cornelius is even there unless Shakespeare just had to create a role for someone but didn't want to actually give him lines. Anyway, the messenger says he has reached the uncle of Fortinbras. The uncle thought Fortinbras was raising an army to attack Poland and had no idea it was actually to attack Denmark. The uncle apologizes and forces his nephew, Fortinbras, to swear he will never attack Denmark. The uncle gives Fortinbras $60,000 a year as a salary and puts him in charge of the army to attack Poland and request that Denmark allows the Norwegian army to pass through Denmark peacefully. The thot King is happy for the news and says he will reply later to the uncle of Fortinbras' request. They don't explicitly say it, but I assume he is the actual ruler of Norway.

Old man Polonius starts explaining his theory on why Hamlet is 15 rolls short of a dozen. He thinks it's because Hamlet is "madly in love" with his daughter Ophelia. He reads a note from Hamlet to prove his theory. It starts out saying *"most beautified Ophelia"*, which Polonius thinks is a crude phrase and then goes on to read *"in her excellent white bosom"* and says nothing about that. So, talking about her beauty is gross, but talking about her breast is okay? Polonius has issues.

He reads more of the letter and tells thot King and Queen that he knew Hamlet was in love with Ophelia before she told him (yeah right) and that he told Ophelia to stop dating Hamlet because she was below his class in society and if he didn't tell her that what would the thot King and Queen think of him? Thot King ask the Queen if she thinks it is possible Hamlet is tweet short of a twitter over Ophelia and she thinks it is possible. Polonius ask the thot King when he can remember him being wrong. The thot King can't remember a time. Polonius then comes up with this plan to prove his theory. Polonius is going to use Ophelia as bait. She is going to find Hamlet and get him to confess his love and his coo cooness to her while Polonius and thot King hide behind his curtains or something. Thot King likes the idea and he and the Queen leave.

Hamlet enters reading and wandering around the stage. Polonius approaches Hamlet asking how he is doing. Hamlet doesn't like Polonius apparently and just messes with him the entire scene. He calls him a fishmonger, basically a fisher man, and Polonius says he isn't one, then Hamlet returns saying he wishes Polonius was as honest as one. Polonius ask what Hamlet is reading and Hamlet responds "words, words, words". Hamlet tells Polonius that he is reading a book where the author describes how all men age and if Polonius aged backwards, Benjamin Button style, then they would be the same age. Just a general smart ass to Polonius. It's funny. Polonius the whole time keeps thinking Hamlet is referencing his daughter to him. Polonius eventually leaves, and Guildenstern and Rosencrantz enter.

Hamlet greets Guildenstern and Rosencrantz very warmly. They are good friends and you can tell by their interaction. They joke, they play, they mess with each other. They start joking that Guildenstern and Rosencrantz are living in Fortune's, or Lady Luck today, vagina, which is weird, but hey that was 13th century Denmark for you. Hamlet then tells them that he feels Denmark is a prison to him and he doesn't know why they would willing go to prison. Guildenstern and Rosencrantz try cheering him up by saying he is too ambitious for Denmark and that is why he is sad here. Hamlet then presses them as to why they have really come to Elsinore. Guildenstern and Rosencrantz are coy about it at first and don't want to answer. They eventually cave and say they are there because the thot King and Queen sent for them. Hamlet says he knows why, and they should all agree to his theory or Guildenstern and Rosencrantz may violate some oath or loyalty to the thot King and Queen.

His basic theory is that he has been moping around, being emo and thot King and Queen freaked out, so they sent for his friends. Hamlet goes off on how nothing gives him pleasure anymore. Rosencrantz laughs and says Hamlet won't get any pleasure then from a group of actors he and Guildenstern meet on their way to the castle and convinced to come to the castle to perform for him and the other royals. Hamlet changes tunes and wants to know all about them and why aren't they performing in the city anymore. Rosencrantz tells Hamlet that the city theaters have been taken over by child actors and no one wants to see the adult actors anymore. This greatly confuses Hamlet and wonders if this is a sign of times. He concludes this is just Thot King's Denmark now.

The actors, or players as they are called, enter with Polonius. Hamlet continues to give Polonius a hard time and quotes a line with a random daughter in it. Polonius thinks it is a reference to Ophelia and says he has a lovely daughter. Hamlet doesn't think this make any sense, nothing lovely could come from him basically. Hamlet greets the actors and is overjoyed they have arrived. He implores one of them to perform a monologue about how Pyrrhus killed Priam right there in front of them.

The monologue is about the events that set up mythology of Troy. Basically, Pyrrhus is a fierce warrior who kills everyone, fathers, mothers, daughters, son. He is Troy's version of Kratos, the God of War. Pyrrhus ends up fighting Priam who is an old man and kills him. Hecuba is Priam's wife and watches Pyrrhus hack off her husbands' limbs and runs through the castle very disheveled. It's pretty intense and you should read the entire thing or Brad Pitt should make a prequel to Troy. Polonius interrupts during the actor's monologue and I just picture Hamlet giving him a death stare when he does. The monologue is over, and Hamlet tells Polonius to treat them very well, better than he even deserves. As they are leaving Hamlet ask the lead actor if he could memorize some lines Hamlet is writing and put them in the show. The lead actor says he can do it and leaves.

Hamlet ask Guildenstern and Rosencrantz to leave and they do right away. Hamlet's soliloquy begins. He starts wondering how this actor could be so emotional over people he had never meet. How could he evoke such emotions? If the actor had the same emotions as Hamlet then everyone would be crying, the guilty would confess their crimes, the innocent would be appalled. Hamlet is a very modest person.

He turns it on himself wondering why he hasn't done anything to avenge his father despite being granted permission from heaven to do so. If anyone came up to him and kicked his ass, then he would have to take it because that is what he deserves. Hamlet comes up with a plan. He is going to use the actors to perform a scene that is very similar to how his uncle killed his father and he is going to watch his uncle to see if his uncle reacts in a way that would confirm he did kill his father. Hamlet wonders if the ghost he saw wasn't actually his father but the devil instead trying to trick him. He basically says, whatever, and ends excited about his plan to catch the thot King.

ACT 3
Scene 1 Recap

We start with the thot King and Queen questioning Rosencrantz and Guildenstern about their meeting with Hamlet. They don't really say much, just that he wasn't really that crazy, but something was bothering him. The Queen ask how he treated them and if they were able to get him to enjoy himself. They mention that they found some actors on the side of the road and convinced them to put on a play tonight at the castle and Hamlet was happy about that and wanted them to come see the play. Polonius interjects and says that is true. The thot King and Queen agree to see the play and excuse Rosencrantz and Guildenstern. They leave.

The thot King ask the Queen to leave because he and Polonius are going to act out Polonius plan to see if Hamlet is really mad because of his love for Ophelia. She obliges and leaves. Polonius gives Ophelia some last minute advise and they go hide.

Hamlet enters and gives his famous "To be or not to be" soliloquy. It's basically about him thinking about if he should commit suicide or not and compares death to sleeping, but then wonders what kinds of dreams you would have if you could never wake up. He figures out that people will endure a lot of suffering in life because they are afraid of death and everyone is a coward when it comes to death and committing suicide.

Hamlet sees Ophelia and she greets him. She has old love letters that she wants to give to Hamlet, at first, he rejects them saying they aren't his. She insists they are, and Hamlet starts to question if she is an honest fair person. This confuses Ophelia and she doesn't know what to make of it. Hamlet is obviously mad at Ophelia and berates her throughout the rest of the scene. He tells her to go be a nun or she should go be a prostitute in a whore house. He curses any potential marriage she may have and tells her she will never have kids because no one will ever want her sexually. He gets pretty intense with her and then leaves. Ophelia wonders how Hamlet could of gone from such a man to what he is now, and she is an idiot forever thinking she would be loved by him.

The thot King and Polonius enter. Thot King doesn't think Hamlet loved Ophelia at all from their interaction but is over figuring it out. He wants to send him to England to be an emissary, hoping the change of scenery will make Hamlet return to normal. Polonius refusing to admit he was wrong thinks that Hamlet's madness started with his love for Ophelia. He asks the thot King to wait on sending Hamlet to England until after the play, so the Queen can speak to Hamlet and see if she can find out why he is crazy while Polonius hides and listens. The thot King agrees, and the scene ends.

Scene 2 Recap

This is a fun scene, one of the more famous scenes in Hamlet. The play within a play. We start with Hamlet giving directing notes to one of the actors. He wants it perfect, but it's apparent he would be an annoying director irl. Polonius, Guildenstern, and Rosencrantz enter, and Hamlet immediately ask if the thot King and Queen will be coming to see the show. Polonius confirms he is and then ask all three to ensure the actors will be ready when thot King and Queen arrive.

Horatio enters. Hamlet greets him and then tells Horatio he was not flirting or flattering him, I don't understand the difference and I don't think there is one. Anyway, Hamlet says there is no point to flirt with the poor as you can't get anything from them, but it is better to flirt with the rich as they may give you things. He then brings it back to Horatio telling him he is a good person and he respects him a lot. Hamlet ends wondering if the ghost they saw was actually his fathers or a demon sent from hell to trick him. He asks Horatio to watch his uncle during the play to see if he gives away his guilt. Horatio agrees and everyone else enters.

Thot King ask how Hamlet is doing and Hamlet gives a nonsense answer. It confuses thot King as was its intention. Hamlet turns to Polonius and makes fun of him directly to his face without Polonius noticing. He truly does not like him. Hamlet cozies up to Ophelia and is very flirty or flattering to her. No, he is straight up hitting on her. He asks to put his head in between her legs and then plays it off. He gets upset when he starts talking about his father dying 2 hours ago. Ophelia reminds him it was 4 months. Hamlet is relieved because it means when you die there is a chance someone will remember you for a whole 6 months.

The actors enter and perform a silent scene where they reenact the supposed death of Hamlet's father. Ophelia and Hamlet start talking during the scene, which is quite rude. Hamlet talks a lot during the play, and no one tells him to shut up. Hamlet uses that time to flirt with Ophelia some more. The actors resume their performance. It's a very sweet scene where the King knows he is dying, and the Queen says she could never love another. The King tries to convince her that she may one day but the Queen refuses to believe. It's all very meta.

Hamlet ask the real Queen how she likes the play and she say her famous line "The lady doth protest too much, methinks." This is what Hamlet wanted to hear. The thot King asks the name of this play and Hamlet says it is called "The Mousetrap". He explains the rest of the play and pronounces that the thot King and himself have nothing to worry about, only the guilty would feel bad. The play continues with Lucianus coming in and poisoning the King in the ear with poison in the garden. Hamlet loudly ask how anyone could ever do such a thing. At that point, the thot King leaves.

Everyone leaves except Horatio and Hamlet. They confirm to each other that the thot King did get weird when the play was going on meaning the ghost was telling the truth. Guildenstern and Rosencrantz enter. Hamlet is being coy and aloof with Guildenstern when Guildenstern starts telling Hamlet that his mother requested to have a talk with him. Rosencrantz steps in and tries to diffuse the situation. He does ask Hamlet if they are still bros. Hamlet resoundingly says yes. Rosencrantz is feeling all of the feels and presses to find out why Hamlet has been acting so odd lately. Hamlet is about to explain when actors enter bringing with them recorders. Now Hamlet may be the biggest fan of recorders in all of history. He absolutely loves them.

He takes one and turns to Guildenstern asking him to play one. Guildenstern is clear that he cannot, but Hamlet persist. When Guildenstern proclaims, he doesn't have the skill, Hamlet unloads on him, asking him why he thought Guildenstern could play Hamlet. Is Hamlet a more useless instrument than a recorder? Guildenstern does not answer because Polonius enters. Hamlet turns his attention to Polonius and immediately starts picking on him. Polonius tells Hamlet his mother has requested him to visit her. Hamlet agrees and tells them he will be there shortly. He ends the scene being very emo, wondering what would happen if he drank blood, and tells himself that he loves his mother dearly, but he is going to have to go off on her. It is something he is not comfortable doing, but feels he has to do it.

Scene 3 Recap

Thot King still mad from the play about himself, if we are being honest, starts the scene with Rosencrantz and Guildenstern. He tells them he does not like Hamlet anymore and is sending them all to England because he will not let the kid who is one chicken nugget shy of a happy meal run freely around the castle. Guildenstern is nice and polite as usual. Rosencrantz goes off saying an individual is naturally protected from being annoyed but kings not so much. They are like a mountain of machinery, if one clog clogs then the entire collection of clogs clog and the king is no more. You have to love him. He doesn't give a flying duck, sorry auto corrects. They leave, and Polonius enters.

Polonius tells the thot King that he is going straight to the Queen's room and will be hiding when Hamlet gets there and will make sure the Queen finds out why Hamlet is crazy like a fox, and then kisses his ass and leaves, not literally.

The thot King confess to the murder of his brother. If there was any doubt left as if he did it or not, his soliloquy ends that. To be fair, it does seem that he is regretting the murder of his brother. To be fairer, it does seem like he is regretting that he can't be forgiven for the murder of his brother while he is king. He doesn't know how he can be forgiven when he is still benefiting from the crime. I don't have answers for him, or do I want to give answers to him even if I had them. The dude deserves to suffer. He decides to pray as that is his only option.

Hamlet enters and sees the thot King praying. He takes out his sword and is about to kill the thot King when he pauses. He realizes that everyone will just think he killed him to become king and not because he was seeking his revenge. It's annoying for sure, especially since the thot king is confessing and may receive a "get out of hell free" card if he is killed right then. Hamlet resolves not to kill him but to wait until he can kill the thot king when he can know for sure he won't be going to heaven, but straight to hell instead. He leaves and the thot king stops praying.

Scene 4 Recap

Act 3 keeps on delivering the hits. This is a very memorable scene so let's bring it. Polonius, the brilliant game maker, is with the Queen to enact his plan of hiding behind a wall rug while the Queen finds the truth about Hamlet's coocooness. Hamlet enters, and Polonius hides right away.

The Queen immediately tells Hamlet that he has offended his "father". Hamlet retorts saying that she is the one who has offended HIS father. The argument immediate goes off the rails and they start getting mad at each other until the Queen fears that Hamlet will murder here right there and calls for help. Polonius, whose mind rivalries Eisenstein, starts yelling for help behind the tapestry. Hamlet not knowing who it is kills the rat behind the curtain. The Queen freaks out and Hamlet hopes he just killed the king. He becomes disappointed when he finds out that it is just Polonius.

At this moment I would like to give a short eulogy, or how Derek Zoolander says a eugoogooly, for the recent decease. Polonius, you were stupid and mean to your daughter and weird to your son and stupid, and I didn't like you as a character, and I hope you were not based on a real person, but if you were than I take comfort that both you and that real person are now dead. The end.

    Okay, moving on. Hamlet barely gives the death of Polonius a second thought and turns back on his mother. She asks what she has done to deserve such mean words from her son. Hamlet claps back at her with such viciousness that I felt it when I read it. Seriously, memorize the translation I wrote and when someone is mean to you tell them it and they will be knocked unconscious with your words. The Queen doesn't know how to take it, so Hamlet explains further.

    He goes into a 30-line monologue comparing his father to his uncle and continues to ask his mother how she could of went from a hunk to a flunk. The Queen ask for him to stop, that she can't take it anymore, but Hamlet will not stop. He continues to tear into her until the Ghost King comes in and reminds him that he is not supposed to take it out on his mother. Hamlet listens and after 130 lines of him basically ripping his mother a new one says "Hey, how's it going?" This confuses the Queen and she ask what he is looking at and who he is talking to. Now Hamlet is confused and ask if she can see the Ghost King. She cannot. Hamlet doesn't understand how she cannot but before he can figure out a reason the Ghost King leaves.

    Now is Hamlet mad? Did he just hallucinate the ghost? Or do ghost in Denmark have the power to show themselves only to who they want? We already established they can talk freely, which is not usual for ghost. So maybe they have this extra power or maybe Hamlet is a screen door on a submarine. Hamlet confesses he is not crazy and has been playing crazy this whole time and tells his mother that she needs to repent her sins and not to commit more in the future. The Queen says he has cut her heart in two. Hamlet gives very sensible advice, throw the bad part away and live a pure life with the good half. His anger turns towards his uncle eventually asking his mother not to sleep with him again, but almost immediately ask her to actually continue sleeping with him, so she can convince the thot King that Hamlet is not crazy but just acting. She agrees reluctantly. He reminds her that he is supposed to go to England and then drags the dead Polonius into the next room wishing her a good night.

Act 4
Scene 1 Recap

The next 4 scenes are all short and I will make these recaps as short as I can.

The Queen tells the thot King that Hamlet killed Polonius and that he dragged the body out of her room. The thot King blames himself for not locking Hamlet up in a looney bin by now and feels his love for him prevented him from doing so. He calls in Rosencrantz and Guildenstern and tells them what Hamlet did and ask them to find him and not to harm him, but to also find the body and bring it to the chapel. The thot King concludes he has to speak to his advisors on how to minimize the damage done and is now fully committed to sending Hamlet to England ASAP.

Scene 2 Recap

Hamlet is hiding Polonius' body when Rosencrantz and Guildenstern with some guards show up to ruin the fun. Rosencrantz ask Hamlet where the body is, so they can take it to the chapel. Hamlet doesn't want to answer and calls out Rosencrantz for playing both sides, friend to him and informant to the thot King. Hamlet continues to refuse to say where the body is, and Rosencrantz says he has to go with them to the thot King. Hamlet agrees only if they can catch him, forcing them to catch him.

Scene 3 Recap

The thot King is telling random people in the room that he sent for Hamlet and that he has to be careful how he punishes him for he is loved by the people. Rosencrantz enters and tells the thot King that Hamlet is just outside, but he would not tell them where the body is. The King tells Rosencrantz to bring in Hamlet and asks Hamlet where the body of Polonius is. Hamlet responds that he is at dinner, only he is the meal and not eating. He is being eaten by worms for worms eat kings and beggars and to a worm there is no difference. Hamlet finds this thought amusing. The thot King does not and ask again where Polonius is. Hamlet responds this time that he is probably in heaven and if not, he is in hell, but if they look and cannot find him in either place, they should check under the stairs.

The thot King informs Hamlet that because of what he did then he has to go to England. Hamlet calls the thot King his mother and explains that if they are man and wife then they are the same and he can call him mother if he wants. Hamlet leaves happily, and the thot King commands Hamlet is followed and brought to the ship quickly. He gets real evil and reveals that he has asked the King of England to kill Hamlet when he arrives.

Scene 4 Recap

Fortinbras is back. He was briefly mentioned in Act One where he wanted to attack Denmark for his father losing some of the land but was convinced by his uncle to attack Poland again. Well, he showed up with an army wanting permission to march through Denmark. He sends his Captain to deliver the news to the thot King. Along the way, the Captain meets Hamlet who questions him about the sudden foreign army in Denmark. The Captain tells Hamlet that there are 2,000 soldiers whose goal is to attack a small worthless piece of land in Poland that no one should want, but everyone must have. Poland has already built buildings to protect it and Fortinbras means to possess it. Hamlet thanks him for his honesty and tells his captives that he will catch up to them after he speaks his thoughts out loud to himself alone. They agree for some reason and leave Hamlet.

Hamlet wonders how everything is preventing him from fulfilling his revenge and all he does is eat and sleep. What good is a man who does that? God made us to be more than just animals. He looks at the army and is amazed that this stupid boy Fortinbras can command an army and he cannot command his own revenge. It inspires him to complete his revenge and swears he will only think of it going forward.

Scene 5 Recap

Ophelia is outside the Queen's chambers insisting on seeing her. The Queen does not want to see her. The "gentlemen", which is such a generic name for a character tells the Queen that Ophelia is not only a nut case, but she is a pathetic sad nut case. Horatio fears that she may spread her crazy ideas to others, and it is best the Queen sees her. The Queen agrees, and Ophelia enters.

Ophelia sings most of her lines in this scene. It is quickly determined she has lost her mind due to her father's death. Shakespeare also uses Ophelia to demonstrate what real madness looks like to contrast what Hamlet has been doing. Ophelia is really cray cray, while Hamlet may have only been just cray. The Queen gets nothing out of Ophelia when the thot King enters. He tries finding anything out from her, but she just replies with crazy song after crazy song. He believes too that her mind went gonzo because of her father being killed by her former bae. Ophelia eventually wanders off and the thot King turns to the Queen. He recaps the last few scenes. Polonius is dead, Hamlet is banished, and oh Laertes, Polonius' son, has returned from France and Act One.

They hear a noise from outside and a messenger enters very afraid of what is outside. A mob has gathered all trying to get it and chanting "Laertes for King!" The thot King calmly says, "The doors are broken." And Laertes strolls in heroically. I would like to think after he enters his hands go to his hips and he looks off to the distance while wind blows his hair.

Laertes goes straight to the thot King and demands to know where his father is. Thot King informs him that his father died, the Queen quickly includes that the thot King did not kill him. Laertes says nothing will stop his revenge, not even heaven or hell. Laertes wants to know how his father died and he will have his revenge. Thot King calms down Laertes a little. Ophelia wanders back into the scene singing, of course. Laertes, her brother, cannot believe what has happened to her and vows revenge again. It's almost to the point that if Laertes went through a drive thru and they gave him the wrong order he would vow revenge until he got the correct order. *"I will seek my revenge on Starbucks for not giving me my add shot!"*

Anyway, Laertes tries talking to Ophelia, but she doesn't listen. She sings and talks about flowers and who gets what and who will wear what. It's all very crazy and she wanders away again. Thot King asks Laertes if he would be willing to gather his wisest friends and they will determine if the thot King is guilty not of Polonius' death and if he is then Laertes will get the entire kingdom, but if he is innocent than they will find the true killer together. Laertes agrees and they both leave.

Scene 6 Recap

A generic gentleman comes up to Horatio and informs him that some sailors have letters for him. Horatio says to bring them in and the generic g'man does. The sailor tells Horatio that he has letters for from the ambassador that was travelling to England. Horatio opens the letters and reads. The letter is from Hamlet.

Hamlet states that on the second day of their voyage they were attacked by pirates. During the fight he was taken prisoner. The pirates figured out who he was and want him to do them a favor. Basically, Hamlet writes a few letters to the thot King and Horatio to gives the sailors or pirates if we are being honest, some money, sending them to the thot King while Horatio quickly comes to greet Hamlet. Horatio does so, and the scene ends.

Scene 7 Recap

We have resumed the normal length scenes, but not a lot happens in this scene. The thot King and Laertes are hanging out talking about how much they hate Hamlet. The thot King first tells Laertes that he has to know by now that he did not kill his father. Laertes agrees but wonders why the thot King didn't imprison Hamlet as soon as he found out what he did. Thot King said it was for 2 reasons. 1 the Queen would of freaked out and he loves her too much to cause her pain. 2, the people love Hamlet so much that it would of come back to haunt the thot King if he did anything to Hamlet. Laertes is like "cool so because the people like Hamlet I have a dead father and a crazy sister. That's rad." The thot King tells Laertes not to worry so much and is about to tell Laertes he can be his daddy now when a messenger interrupts.

The messenger has a note from Hamlet saying he is returning to the castle and has requested a meeting with the thot King. Laertes makes sure it is Hamlet who wrote it and the thot King confirms it is Hamlet's handwriting. The thot King tells Laertes about this Norman, Lamord, who has excellent riding skills on a horse and that he praised Laertes, which made Hamlet jealous. Laertes says "cool, so what?" The thot King ask if Laertes loved his father. Laertes is getting annoyed with the thot King and wants to know where all of this is going. The thot King reveals his plan. He first asks Laertes if he is willing to show how much he loved his father and what he would do to Hamlet if he had the chance. Laertes says he would cut his throat in the church, which is a little harsh if you ask me. Thot King isn't fazed by this, because he is a horrible person, and continues to tell his plan.

When Hamlet returns, they will announce that Laertes is back and remind everyone how much that Norman liked Laertes and how skillful Hamlet thought he was with a sword. He will then ask Hamlet to practice and while they are practicing Laertes will ask Hamlet to duel to avenge his father. Laertes likes the plan but decides to add a little spice to the plan. He brought this poison from probably the same guy who sold Romeo his poison and plans on dipping his sword in it. If Laertes scratches Hamlet at all then he will die. Thot King likes the plan but wants a backup plan as well. He is all for the poisoned sword but also wants to add the poison to a cup and entice Hamlet to drink from it. This way they are sure they will kill Hamlet, and nothing could go wrong. No one will accidentally drink from the cup. Nope.

    The Queen enters and tells Laertes that Ophelia has drowned. She was out by a willow gathering flowers, as she was known to do. She decided to hang some of the flowers from a tree branch and fell into the water. She didn't try to swim out and eventually her clothes became too heavy and she drowned. Laertes is kinda upset, but also isn't really as much as he should be and leaves. Thot King tells the Queen they should leave too.

Act 5
Scene 1 Recap

We start with 2 gravediggers digging the grave for Ophelia. In the play they are called Gravedigger and Other, but I will call them GD and Bob for the purpose of this recap. GD is very woke. He first starts asking why they are digging the grave if Ophelia committed suicide. Back then, if you committed suicide you were not allowed to be buried on holy ground, and they didn't take mental illness into account. Bob says the coroner ruled her death an accident, but GD doesn't buy it. He starts using logic to disprove the ruling because he knows she intentionally drowned. Bob is just along for the ride and let's GD have his say. GD eventually ask Bob to go get them some alcohol to drink and Bob leaves.

Hamlet and Horatio enter. The see GD singing while digging the grave and Hamlet is offended by it. Horatio tells him that GD isn't thinking about the solemn nature of his work, but that it is just a job to him. Hamlet decides to approach and talk to GD. Now GD is a bit of a smart ass and won't directly answer any of Hamlet's questions. Hamlet tries finding out who's grave it is but can't. GD mentions that he has been working as a gravedigger since Hamlet was born, but that doesn't matter now since Hamlet is crazy and shipped off to England. Hamlet intrigued starts asking GD about himself. Hamlet finds out that GD doesn't know why he went crazy, only that he did. Hamlet starts asking about how long a person will stay in the grave before they decompose. GD says it depends if they were rotten before they were put in the grave or not. It's funny. He is a funny character.

GD hands Hamlet a skull and tells him that it is Yorick and then we get the iconic picture of Hamlet holding up a skull saying "Yorick! I knew him well" ...well that was before the Mandela effect changed the line. Hamlet goes full emo morbid as he tends to do and wonders what the point of life is if all that happens is you turn to dust.

The King, Queen, Laertes, and extras enter. They bring the body of Ophelia to be laid to rest. Laertes ask the minister what else needs to happen now that they are at the grave and the minister doesn't want to do anything else because Ophelia killed herself. Laertes is not too happy with that and jumps into the grave of Ophelia hugging her and telling them to bury them both.

Hamlet doesn't want to be out done and comes out saying that he loved her more than anyone else. Laertes starts to strangle Hamlet, literally choke him, and not the good kind of choking either. However, Hamlet is still able to get off 5 lines of dialogue during it. They are separated, and Hamlet continues to express his love for Ophelia. He didn't know she died and is really torn up about it. He eventually can't take it anymore and leaves. The Thot King ask Horatio to follow and reminds Laertes that they have a plan for Hamlet and all he has to do is wait until the next scene to see it carried out.

Scene 2 Recap

Oh Nellie, are you ready for this? We start with Hamlet and Horatio hanging out. Hamlet begins to tell Horatio the story of his time on the ship that was bound for England. Hamlet wakes up one night, not being able to sleep, and decides to walk around the ship. He finds a letter from the thot King to England telling them to kill Hamlet right away. Horatio is in disbelief and Hamlet hands him the original

...tter while telling him what he did next. Hamlet, not wanting to be killed, decides to write a new letter the style of the thot King but instead of him being the target he changes it to Rosencrantz and Guildenstern instead. Hamlet even has an old seal that looks like the King's seal to make it look super official. Horatio ask if he really sent Rosencrantz and Guildenstern to die. Hamlet says he doesn't think about them anymore. They loved working for the thot King and spying on him. So, they can go to hell for all he cares. Horatio tells Hamlet that is very kingly of him.

    Osric enters. He is a stupid man and Hamlet makes fun of him a lot. He is a lot like Polonius and Hamlet treats him as such. There is a little comic bit where Hamlet keeps telling Osric to put on his hat. Osric doesn't want to because it's hot, but Hamlet insist. Anyway, Osric was sent by the thot King to tell Hamlet that the thot King bet Hamlet could not beat Laertes in a friendly sword fight. He waged 4 African horses against 4 French swords and daggers. Osric goes on to tell Hamlet how great a person and swordsman Laertes is. Hamlet agrees but goes over the top with his praise. So much that he is mocking Laertes, but Osric doesn't get the joke and thinks Hamlet is serious. After much back and forth, Osric finally ask Hamlet if he will duel and Hamlet agrees. Osric exits.

    A Lord enters and tells Hamlet that the thot King has received news that Hamlet intends to duel with Laertes for the bet and ask if Hamlet is ready for the duel. Hamlet says he is ready now, if Laertes is, and if Laertes is not ready now then Hamlet will be ready when he is. The Lord tells Hamlet that both the Queen and the thot King are coming down now to watch the duel and exits.

    Horatio tells Hamlet that he does not think he can win, and Laertes is actually a good fighter. Hamlet tells Horatio that he has been practicing the entire time since Laertes has been in France and he is the goat at swordplay.

    A bunch of people enter, and the stage is set for the duel. The thot King ask Hamlet to shake hands with Laertes. Hamlet does and immediately apologies for killing his father. He blames his mental illness on his father's death and claims that he should not take any blame but is a victim himself. Laertes accepts the apology but says he has to double check first if accepting the apology means his honor won't be tarnished. The thot King says that if Hamlet strikes first or second or if Laertes gets the first two and Hamlet the third then he will win a massive pearl and the thot King will drink to his health. Remember he plans on poisoning the drink. They duel.

    Hamlet nails the first hit right away. The thot King then drinks some wine and drops the poisoned pearl into the wine and offers it to Hamlet. Hamlet denies the wine and says he will keep dueling. Hamlet immediately gets the second hit. The thot King tells the Queen he thinks their son will win and she, for some reason, says Hamlet is fat and out of breath. She picks up the poisoned wine and cheers to Hamlet and drinks. The thot King knows that the Queen is now poisoned. She offered Hamlet a drink, but he refuses again. She instead wipes his sweaty forehead. Laertes tells the thot King he will hit Hamlet now and the thot King doubts it will happen. Laertes begins to have second doubts about their plan but goes forward away.

    Laertes hits Hamlet and then they grab each other, and, in the fight, they drop their swords, picking up each other swords. Laertes is then struck by his own sword, which was poisoned as well. Now let's pause. The Queen is poisoned from wine. Hamlet and Laertes are now both poisoned from the swords. The Queen falls down and so does Laertes. Laertes says that he has been killed by his own hand. Hamlet ask how the Queen is and the thot King says he fainted at the sight of blood. The Queen says no, was not that, it was poisoned. The cup was poisoned! She dies. Hamlet calls for all of the doors to be locked and no one to leave the room. Laertes confesses that he is to blame, and that Hamlet is also poisoned. He is holding the cause of his poison in his hand. He puts all of the blame of the poison on the thot King.

Hamlet looks at the poison sword and stabs the thot King in the chest. Everyone is shooked, but Hamlet isn't done yet. He grabs the wine cup and forces the thot King to drink the poison. The thot King dies. Laertes says the thot King got what he deserved and dies himself. Within 20 lines, the Queen, Laertes, and the thot King all die.

Hamlet tells the dead Laertes he forgives him and will see him soon in the afterlife. He looks over the crowd and tells them that he knows things that would blow their mind, but death waits for no one. Hamlet turns to Horatio and tells him to live and tell his story. Horatio says no one would ever believe him and that there is some poison left that he can drink. Hamlet refuses and demands Horatio give him the cup. Horatio refuses at first, but gives in. Hamlet tells him again to tell everyone his story and they hear a loud noise. Osric says it is Fortinbras and an ambassador from England arriving.

Hamlet tells Horatio he will not live to see them, but he wants Fortinbras to be king and dies himself. Fortinbras with the Ambassador enter and are obviously shocked at what they see. Horatio tells them they he can tell them a story of misery, sadness, and tragedy they won't believe. Fortinbras tells him to wait until all of the nobles can be assembled, but he thinks he will assume the throne. Horatio tells him that Hamlet thought the same thing before he died. Fortinbras declares that Hamlet should be treated like a hero solider who has fallen in battle and commands his body to be carried out. And must like the end of Gladiator they carry Hamlet's body off stage leaving the king.

And that is how Hamlet ends. Everyone dies. Here is their order.
1. Old King Hamlet dies before the play begins, by poison in the garden.
2. Polonius dies by Hamlet stabbing him in the Queen's room.
3. Ophelia dies by drowning in a pond.
4. The Queen dies by drinking poison.
5. The thot King dies by being stabbed by Hamlet and then drowned on poison.
6. Laertes dies by a poisoned tipped sword in a duel with Hamlet.
7. Hamlet dies by a poisoned tipped sword in a duel with Laertes.
8. Rosencrantz and Guildenstern are confirmed dead by the England Ambassador, but also because Hamlet ordered their death.

I hoped you enjoyed Hamlet. It got real intense real fast at the end, but that's Shakespeare. If you enjoyed this play and/or this translation/modernization look for others in this series. We will eventually have all of Shakespeare's play formatted in this style. Read the Bard and you will probably be the coolest kid in school. Until next time.

People also ask

All of these questions come from Google. All answers are original.

Why did Hamlet not become king after his father died?

He was away at school in Germany. The play is set in the 1300's. It took forever for any message to travel any distance. Hamlet was at school, got the message, left and headed straight to Elsinore, Denmark. When he arrived, his Uncle had already seized the throne and married his mother.

Why is Hamlet upset at the start of the play?

Dude, I think you would be upset if your father died, your mother married your Uncle, and your Uncle took your throne for himself.

How old Is Hamlet at the beginning of the play?

Depends on who plays Hamlet in the production. You will have to ask them. No seriously, we don't learn his age until Act 5 when the Gravedigger say he has been a gravedigger since Hamlet was born 30 years ago.

Does Hamlet want to be king?

It's good to King, why would he not want to be one? Of course, he wants to be king, you noob.

Who is King Claudius in Hamlet?

A rat bastard snake thot who steals Hamlet's throne, married his mother, and murders his father He is also Hamlet's Uncle.

Where did Laertes go in Hamlet?

He went to Paris to be a young noble and to study music.

Who is Ophelia?

Hamlet's bae. Laertes' sis. Polonius' daughter. And not a very good swimmer.

Who is the Hamlet?

That's an odd question. We only assume the answer is Hamton from Tiny Tunes when he played Hamlet. Otherwise, the answer is Sir Kenneth Branagh.

At what age did Hamlet die?

All of Hamlet takes place within a year. He was 30 when the play started. We don't see him celebrate his birthday. So, we assume he was 30 when he died, but he could have been 31.

How do Rosencrantz and Guildenstern die?

They died off stage when they arrive in English. Nowhere is it stated how they die but we like to assume they were killed in a knife fight with a bear.

Is Hamlet a teenager?

Yes, he was when he was 13-19, but he was not a teenager in the play. You are thinking of Romeo.

How long ago was Hamlet written?

No one really knows exactly when. It is assumed it was written in 1601 because of the reference to the children gaining popularity in live theatre. This was known as **The War of the Theatres**. We know it was first published in 1603.

Who is Hamlet's brother?

That's a trick question and if you are ever asked then immediately smack the person who asked Hamlet has no brother, but his dad is also named Hamlet and his brother is Claudius. Hamlet's dad's name is only referenced once in the play. So, it is a tricky question.

Who is the ghost in Hamlet?

Hamlet. Hamlet is the ghost in Hamlet. See we can give tricky answers too. Hamlet's dad, the murdered King, is named Hamlet. The answer is either the murder King of Denmark, Hamlet's dad, or simply Hamlet.

Who does Gertrude marry in Hamlet?

A straight up rat bastard snake thot named Claudius. Claudius is Gertrude's brother-in-law by marriage and Hamlet's uncle.

Is Laertes a God?

Sure, why not. There isn't any evidence that says otherwise, besides Laertes dying of poison and losing a duel to Hamlet.

Why did Hamlet kill Polonius?

Because Polonius was an idiot. Hamlet did not know it was Polonius when he killed him. Polonius was hiding behind a curtain and couldn't keep his mouth shut. When Hamlet was disrespecting his mother, Polonius freaked out and started yelling. Hamlet thought he was, hopefully, the King and stabbed through the tapestry killing Polonius pretty much instantly.

How does Hamlet kill Claudius?

In maybe one of the most bad ass ways possible. First, in front of everyone, he rams his sword through Claudius' heart and then proceeds to try and drown him with poisoned wine.

What is Ophelia's syndrome?

Something that is no good. It is a reference to Hodgkin lymphoma.

What is the main story line of Hamlet?

Seriously, after 20 pages you are now just asking that? Read this entire thing again.

What is a hamlet town?

A town filled with people trying to murder their uncles.

Is Hamlet a novel?

No, it is a play. You should read more plays. They are way better than novels.

How old was William Shakespeare when he married Anne Hathaway?

The answer they teach you in school is 18 yrs. old. Anne Hathaway was 26. Here is the real answer. Shakespeare and Anne Hathaway are immortal. They have been alive since at least the 1500's but probably older. After Shakespeare had his career in theater, they laid low until 1999 when Anne Hathaway decided to start acting again. She kept her original name while William Shakespeare changed his name to Adam Shulman. They announced they were married in 2012 when "Adam" was "31".

Here is photographic evidence supporting my case.

How did Shakespeare die?

I think we just established that he did not die. He is still alive. History did not record the reason for his death outside of maybe he drank too much and died of a fever.

What was Shakespeare's Theatre called?

He worked at The Globe and at The Rose.

Who were Shakespeare's plays performed for?

Everyone. He was not exclusive. He wanted everyone to enjoy his plays, just like we do.

Who designed the original Globe Theatre?

The answer is not known so we are going to go with Thor.

Who performed in Shakespeare's plays?

...actors??

Who was England's Queen during the majority of Shakespeare's life?

Queen Elizabeth

Did Shakespeare have a happy childhood?

Considering it was at least 500 years ago and he didn't die during his childhood then we will say yes it was happy. However, remember no one knows when Shakespeare was born and under what name. We assume he was one of the original druids that built Stonehenge.

Who played the female roles in the play?

When it was originally performed it was done by men.

Is The Lion King based on Hamlet?

It is very similar to Hamlet but there are many differences in it. The real question you should ask and google is "Is the Lion King based on Kimba the White Lion?"

Where was Hamlet first staged?

London, England

Who was on the throne when Hamlet was written?

Queen Elizabeth

Who dies in Hamlet?

Pretty much everyone. King Hamlet, Polonius, Ophelia, Rosencrantz and Guildenstern, Laertes, Gertrude, Claudius, and Hamlet, as well as many sailors and pirates.

What is odd about Shakespeare's birthday?

No birth records exist because he was born in druid times and is still alive today.

What modern day stories and movies are believed to be based on the story of Hamlet?

A lot of stories have paid homage to Hamlet, but the most notable is Kimba the White Lion, sorry we mean The Lion King.

Who Killed Hamlet?

You could say Hamlet killed himself by being obsessed with revenge. You can say Claudius killed him by having Laertes' sword dipped in poison, but it was Laertes who stabbed Hamlet with the poisoned sword.

Who killed Hamlet's father?

His rat bastard snake thot of a brother, Claudius.

Who killed Claudius in Hamlet?

Hamlet killed Claudius in Hamlet.

Who is Hamlet's girlfriend?

Ophelia would be the closest thing to a girlfriend to Hamlet.

Did Shakespeare ever perform in his own plays?

It is believed that he did perform in his own plays but there is no direct evidence for that. We do know Adam Shulman, the name Shakespeare goes by nowadays, is an actor and has been in a few things

Made in United States
Troutdale, OR
05/24/2024